Just for Girls

Written by Sarah Delmege
Illustrated by Lee Wildish

PaRragon

Bath · New York · Singapore · Hong Kong · Cologne · Delhi · Melbourne

First published by Parragon in 2008
Parragon
Queen Street House
4 Queen Street
Bath BA1 1HE, UK

ISBN 978-1-4075-1571-7

Printed in China

CONTENTS

The changes ahead

Puberty is a time of growth and change. Everyone goes through it. Most girls start puberty between the ages of 8 and 13 and it usually ends when your body has reached its adult height and size, around ages 15 to 17.

You may be the same age as your friend, but it doesn't mean you'll start developing at the same time. This can be difficult and embarrassing for both of you, but you will both reach the same stage eventually.

What's next?

Your body will go through many different changes and these can happen in any order. This list will give you a guide of what to expect:

- ✪ Your breasts develop
- ✪ You will grow taller, heavier, and broader
- ✪ Your hips will develop
- ✪ Pubic hair and hair under your arms and on your legs starts to grow
- ✪ Your periods start

Food for your brain!

Read this book from cover to cover, or just dip into it when you feel like you need some extra info. It's packed full of explanations, diagrams, advice, and real-life stories from other readers. Most of it's embarrassing. Some of it's funny. A little of it is scary.

But when you've finished reading, you should have a good idea of what to expect, an understanding of what's happening to you, and some top tips on avoiding embarrassing situations.

 Fact file

You'll gain weight, and may even double your weight while going through puberty. It's a fact that girls put on more fat than boys do as girls need extra energy later in life.

5

Throughout this book you'll see the following symbols crop up. Here's what they mean:

 Readers' stories — Real–life stories!

 Top tip — Advice from the experts!

 Fact file — The technical stuff!

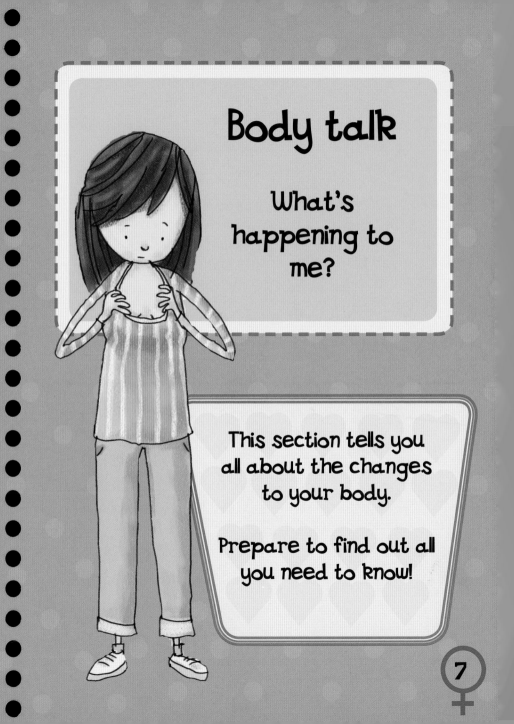

Body talk

What's happening to me?

This section tells you all about the changes to your body.

Prepare to find out all you need to know!

Getting breasts

There's no doubt about it, breasts certainly get a lot of attention. And boy, does this cause a lot of stress for girls who are growing them!

Sadly, you don't have much control over when they start developing. Most girls start growing when they hit double digits, but some girls develop breasts even earlier. Some girls develop at the same time as their friends, whereas others are way ahead of or behind everyone else and end up feeling self-conscious and impatient. One thing's for sure, you're certainly not alone in comparing your chest with the next girl's. It's totally a girl thing.

Why do they start to grow?

Basically, it's in response to the increase of the hormone estrogen in your body, which tells the mammary glands to start growing and also causes cushions of fat to grow and surround these glands. The size of your breasts is all due to whatever size the cushions of fat grow to. And sadly, you have no control over this at all—no matter how many times you do bust exercises. Inside your breasts are a network of milk ducts which are connected to the milk-producing glands. These send milk out of the nipple when the time comes to feed a baby.

Five stages of development

There are roughly five stages of breast development, but everyone goes through them at their own rate. Some girls take a couple of months and can seem to miss out whole stages, while others can take almost ten years to get to the final result. It's frustrating but your body has its own timetable which is all down to hormones and heredity rather than wishful thinking.

Over the next couple of pages these changes are explained in detail.

9

Stages of development

Stage (1)

This usually starts between the ages of 8 to11, but it can be earlier or later. At this point you won't be able to tell anything's going on, but inside your body puberty is beginning. Your ovaries are starting to enlarge and estrogen is beginning to circulate around your body.

Stage (2)

This is the first stage you'll be able to actually see. Your nipples and the surrounding skin—called the areola—get larger and may even get darker in color. The area might feel a little tender or even ache and it may hurt to sleep on your stomach or to wear certain clothes. It's not very comfortable, but don't worry, it's totally normal and nothing to worry about.

Stage ③

At this point, fat deposits start to fill out the area around your nipples and the areola. Your breasts might well start taking on a pointy shape. This is when the size of your breasts is pretty much determined by your body. And you might want to start thinking about wearing a bra at this point.

Stage ④

Some girls skip this stage altogether. But for those of you who don't, you'll see your nipples and areolas get bigger and more pronounced, beginning to form a separate mound at the end of your breasts. Your breasts will begin to fill out and grow larger. If you didn't get your period during Stage 3, you probably will now.

Stage ⑤

What you see now could very well be what you get sizewise, but breast size can change throughout your life. Things like weight change or hormonal factors can have an effect on the size of your breasts. Plus a number of women's breasts will continue to change throughout their twenties.

Shapes and sizes

The thing about breasts is that there's no such thing as a normal shape. Whether they're small, medium, or large, everyone's are different. The thing is to be happy with your own shape. After all, what's not to love, they're part of you!

Your whole body is asymmetrical and a little lop-sided. Take a close look at your eyes and ears, they're not exactly the same are they? Well exactly the same applies to your breasts. With some girls the difference is enough to be noticeable but almost never dramatically so. It's generally a lot less noticeable to other people than you, so if your breasts or your nipples are a little uneven, please don't worry about it. You're really not alone.

★ Top tip

Nipples stick out and can end up rubbing against your clothes. As a result they can end up feeling a little irritated, dry, and cracked, and even bleed a little. If this happens, try wearing soft fabrics or natural fibers.

Some nipples don't stick out at all, instead they appear to stick in. These are known as inverted nipples. Some nipples might go from innies to outies while your breasts are developing. Others just stay that way. Don't worry if yours are like this, lots of girls have them.

You may notice lines appearing on your breasts. When breasts or any part of the body grows fast the skin has to stretch to keep up. Sometimes the skin just isn't elastic enough to do it and as a result purplish lines called stretch marks may appear. These are very common, most women have them. Often they fade with time.

Why are my breasts hurting?

Most girls experience some occasional breast pain, usually before a period or when your breasts are first starting to develop. If the pain is really bad, or it happens at totally irregular times which are not linked to your menstrual cycle, or is much worse in one breast it's worth mentioning it to your doctor.

Bras

Whether or not to wear a bra is an entirely personal decision. A lot of women find they are more comfortable with their breasts supported and like the shape a bra gives them. Wearing the right bra during sports not only stops breasts jiggling, but it can help prevent injury to breast tissue.

Some experts think wearing a bra prevents sagging. They say it can help keep some of the elasticity of the tissue and the ligaments that hold the breast up. But others say over time gravity, wear and tear, motherhood and changes in a woman's size brought on by weight gain and loss make a difference no matter how often you wear a bra.

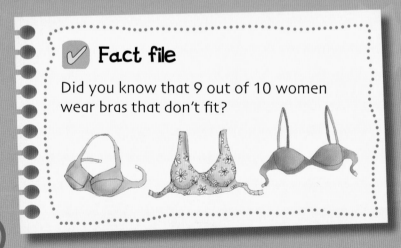

☑ Fact file

Did you know that 9 out of 10 women wear bras that don't fit?

Straps, snaps, bands and cups

Finding the right bra doesn't have to be a problem if you know how to measure yourself. There are two parts to a bra's size; the band size and the cup size. The band size is the part of the bra that runs across your chest and around your back.

The cups are the parts of the bra that hold your breasts. Bras come in lots of different sizes, which are different combinations of the band sizes (shown in numbers—32, 34, 36, etc.) and cup sizes (shown in letters—AA, A, B, C etc).

It's important to get both the band and cup sizes right to make sure your bra fits properly. If you wear a bra that's the wrong size, the bra will feel tight and uncomfortable around your rib cage or it will be too loose. If the bra's too small, it will squeeze your breasts and make them pop out of the sides. And if the cups are too big, they'll wrinkle up which looks totally weird under clothes!

15

Sizing up

So how do you find out your band and cup measurements? The best way is to get yourself measured in a store. But you can find out yourself and the good news is it's really easy, all you need is a tape measure.

Simply run the tape measure just under your breasts, all the way around your back and rib cage. Make sure the tape measure is lying flat on your skin—not so tight that it digs in, but not so loose that it sags down at the back.

Make a note of your measurement and add 5 inches. That's your chest size. If your chest measurement comes out at an odd number (such as 31 inches or 33 inches), simply round up to the next number.

Cup measurement

This time, when you run the tape measure around your body, you're going to take the measurement across the fullest part of your breasts. Now, subtract your chest measurement. If the difference between the two numbers is less than one inch your cup size is AA. If it's one inch, you're an A, two inches you're a B, three inches you're a C, and so on.

How do I know if I have the right size?

When you try on a bra, you'll probably have to make some adjustments to get the perfect fit. Try extending or shortening the band around your chest slightly. The bra's straps allow you to change how the cups fit and support your breasts. When the straps are the right length, a bra should lift your breasts comfortably and the back of the bra will run across your back. You should be able to get one finger under the straps to stop them from digging into your shoulders. Usually petite girls will need to wear their bra straps shorter than girls who are tall.

No matter what the size and shape of your breasts the number one priority in bra-buying is comfort. Try on a few bras to find the one that's right on you. Some girls like cotton, others like the support of underwires. There are minimizer bras for girls who'd like their breasts to look smaller and padded bras, too. No bra is better than another, it's totally a matter of what works best for you.

⭐ Top tip

It's a good idea to try on a T-shirt over a bra to see how it looks under your clothes.

What's on the inside?

Your body will go through many changes that aren't visible as you go through puberty. These changes are all about your body getting ready for the time that you might decide to have a baby.

Where is it and what's it for?

Vagina
This is a canal that leads from the uterus (your womb) and carries menstrual blood and babies. It's roughly about 5 inches long. Your vagina stretches—its walls have many folds which expand and contract.

Cervix
This is the lower part of your uterus.

Uterus
Your uterus, or womb, has walls which are extremely elastic and allow it to grow to many times its original size to accommodate a developing fetus. The lining of the uterus is what helps nourish it. When there's no fetus in the uterus, the lining is shed every month—this is your period.

Fallopian tubes

These two tubes reach from the top of your uterus in either direction to the ovaries. They're about 4 inches long. Their ends are shaped like fringed tunnels, which surround your ovaries but don't actually attach to them. The fallopian tubes carry your eggs (ova) from your ovary to the uterus each month.

Ovaries

You have two ovaries which store all of the potential eggs in your body. These eggs are stored in little pockets called follicles and you are born with hundreds and thousands of them. During puberty, your pituitary gland produces hormones which travel through your bloodstream to your ovaries, causing your follicles to release one egg per month. This is called ovulation.

Here's a handy diagram:

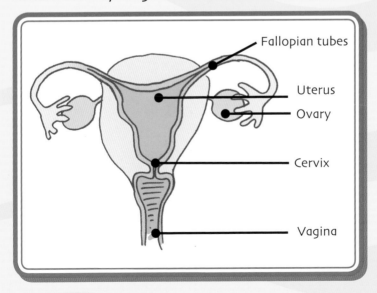

Fallopian tubes

Uterus
Ovary

Cervix

Vagina

19

Your period

Most girls start their period somewhere been 9 and 16 years. When you start has a lot to do with race, diet, weight, and your percentage of body weight.
And a lot of it is hereditary.

A good way to predict when you will start is to ask your mom or sister when they started.

When will it start?

Your first period will usually happen after your breasts have begun to develop and your pubic hair has started to appear. It can be really frustrating if most of your friends start before you. But don't panic, there are plenty of girls who don't get their periods until their late teens.
If you reach 17 and haven't started your period or your breasts or pubic hairs haven't yet appeared, it's probably a good idea to see your doctor.

Your period is totally normal as long as it's somewhat regular. The length of a cycle is usually 21 to 35 days.
28 days is average.

The length of each period is two to eight days (four to six days is average) with bleeding stopping and starting throughout.

Cycles change over the course of your life, depending on things like stress, age, weight gain, or loss or having a baby.

Fact file

Women today have more menstrual periods than ever before, roughly 400 to 500 in a lifetime! This is because girls start menstruating earlier, live longer (thanks to better nutrition and health care,) and have fewer pregnancies.

Dealing with the flow

Most girls deal with their period by using tampons or pads. It's just a matter of finding whatever you are most comfortable with.

Tampons

Tampons absorb blood from inside your vagina. They're made from absorbent cotton, pressed into a cylindrical shape, about the length and thickness of a thumb. They have a string attached to one end for easy removal and they come in a paper or plastic applicator, which makes them easier for you to insert into your vagina.

Tampons come in different sizes of absorbency (words like super-plus or ultra on the packaging usually mean that a tampon is designed for girls whose flow is heavier, whereas slim means it's made for a lighter flow). Again, using these is simply a matter of what you prefer.

How do I insert a tampon?

It's easy to use a tampon but you do need to learn how. Inserting a tampon the first few times can be difficult and uncomfortable. For one thing, you've got to find your vaginal opening. Another tricky part is finding the right angle of insertion. But it's really not as difficult as it sounds. Tampon boxes come with pretty good instructions, so read them carefully and most importantly RELAX! Allow yourself a good amount of time for trial and error—after all this is a new and unfamiliar routine. But it's well worth the effort. It's probably easier to use tampons with applicators while you're getting used to it. Remember to wash your hands before and after using a tampon.

 Fact file

Don't worry that the tampon will get lost in your body. It honestly can't happen! Your cervix (which is the gateway to your uterus) is too small for a tampon to slip through.

23

Pads

Pads come in all shapes and sizes. Super, slender, overnight, with or without wings, maxi, mini . . . pads may seem a bit confusing at first because there are so many different kinds. But with all these choices, it means there really is one that will suit you perfectly. Pads protect you externally.

How do you use them? Most pads have a sticky strip along the bottom. You simply peel off the strip that covers the sticky part, firmly press the pad into the crotch of your underwear (wrapping the wings around the bottom of your panties and sticking them under the crotch if the type you're using has them). Once you've used the pad, simply wrap it in toilet paper and put it in the trashcan, or if you're at school or out somewhere, in the special disposal box that's found in most cubicles.

★ Top tip

Don't try to flush a pad down the toilet—even the lightest kind of pad may block up the toilet and make a huge and embarrassing mess!

Toxic Shock Syndrome

You may have read a printed warning about this on your tampon box. Toxic Shock Syndrome, or TSS, is an extremely rare, but sometimes fatal, bacterial illness that's usually associated with super-absorbent tampons that aren't changed often enough.

Although it's very rare it's important to be aware. If you catch TSS early, it can be cured with antibiotics. Don't panic! TSS is extremely rare and tampons are totally safe if you use them correctly. Be informed, but don't lose sleep over it!

 Fact file

⚙ Change your tampons frequently.

⚙ Use the least absorbent one you can.

⚙ Don't sleep while wearing a tampon (use a pad at night).

⚙ Wash your hands before and after inserting a tampon.

⚙ Only use tampons when you have a period.

PMS

PMS (pre-menstrual syndrome) is the term for a whole bunch of different symptoms that many women experience in the days leading up to their periods. Experts haven't been able to agree on the biological cause of PMS, but your hormonal levels are their lowest in your body during this time. PMS is usually at its worst during the seven days before your period starts, and it disappears once your period begins.

As always, symptoms vary hugely. You might find some of your friends don't get any symptoms at all, while you might get terrible cramps or be supersensitive, weepy, and generally strung out. If you do, try not to shout and scream at some poor innocent person, just because you're feeling short-tempered! It's not smart and it's certainly not fair on the other person.

 ## Top tip

Doing some exercise often helps period pain but if it hurts too much, then resting with a heating pad may also help.

If you're unlucky enough to be among the minority of women who hate this time of the month because you feel sluggish, bloated, irritable, emotional, and generally sore, try to remember that your periods will probably become easier in a few years. In the meantime, you can help ease the symptoms.

Here are some other ideas to make you feel better:

✪ Have a long bath with lavender bubble bath.

✪ Curl up on the sofa with a heating pad.

✪ Eat some of your favorite chocolate.

✪ Allow yourself a good cry and rent out a weepy movie.

Skin

Sometimes it feels like your skin is impossible to manage, especially when you wake up to find a huge zit on the end of your nose. Like your other body parts, hormones play a role in how your skin changes during adolescence.

☑ Fact file

The pores of your skin contain sebaceous (se-bay-shis) glands which make sebum (see-bum), an oil for your hair and skin. Normally, the right amount of sebum is made and everything is totally fine, but sometimes a pore gets clogged up with too much sebum and dead skin cells. Eventually it bursts, becomes inflamed and you end up with a whitehead, blackhead, or pimple.

The reason this is more likely to happen when you're a teenager is because of the influx of androgens (male sex hormones), which makes these places prime zit territory.

Here is a diagram to show what's under your skin's surface:

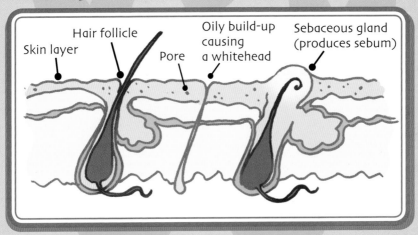

The good news is that there really are ways to prevent and treat common skin problems! Hurrah! And the even better news is that girls' skin troubles are generally not as bad as guys'. It may not feel like it now, but your angry skin will calm down. In the meantime, read on for some handy tips.

Pimples

Here are a few tips on how to prevent breakouts and clear them up as fast as possible.

1 Wash your face twice a day with warm water and a mild soap made to treat acne. Gently massage your face with circular motions. Don't scrub. Over-washing and scrubbing can cause skin to become even more irritated.

2 Don't pop pimples, however tempting it might seem. Popping pimples can push infected material further into the skin and you could end up with more swelling and redness and even scarring. So not a good look.

3 Avoid touching your face with your fingers, as this can spread the bacteria. Make sure you wash your hands before applying anything to your face like make-up.
If you wear glasses or sunglasses, clean them regularly to keep oil from clogging up the pores around your eyes and nose.

⭐ Top tips

If you get acne on your body, try not to wear tight clothes, which don't allow skin to breathe and may cause irritation. It's also a good idea to avoid wearing scarves, headbands, or hats, which can collect dirt and oil.

Always, always, always remove your make-up before you go to bed. And make sure you buy brands that are medicated. Don't forget to replace your make-up regularly—nasty bacteria can build up in make-up over time.

Wash your hair regularly and if it's long tie it back away from your face.

✔️ Fact file

Make sure you protect your skin from the sun. It may seem like a tan covers up your acne, but sunbathing can cause the body to produce extra sebum, which may make your acne worse. Tanning also causes damage to skin that will eventually lead to wrinkles and increase your risk of skin cancer.

Cold sores

Cold sores usually show up as tender pimples on the lips. They're caused by a type of virus (called HSV-1). Once you get this virus, it stays in your body which means you'll probably get cold sores every now and then throughout your life. Here's how to prevent those pesky cold sores from making an appearance:

Cold sores can flare up from things like too much sun, stress, or being under the weather. So make sure you lather on that sun protection lotion, eat well, exercise, and get plenty of sleep.

Don't share stuff like lip balm, toothbrushes, or drinks. The virus that causes cold sores is transmitted through the nose (in mucus—ew!) and the mouth (in saliva).

★ Top tip

If you do get cold sores, here's how to live with them.

 Avoid acidic foods like oranges, tomatoes, and salty, spicy foods.

 However tempting, don't pick 'em. They may bleed or become infected. Yuck!

Food and skin

Many people think that eating chocolate and greasy foods makes your skin break out in pimples so it's always a good idea to pay close attention to what's going on with your body. If you always get pimples after eating a certain thing, cut it out for a while and see what happens.

One of the best things you can do for your skin is to drink tons of water. It flushes out nasty impurities and helps keep your skin hydrated in a healthy way.
And most models and celebrities swear by it.

OK, so let's say you've been drinking water, eating healthy, washing well, exercising, and you never ever sleep with your make-up on. Yet still you wake up with a large pimple on the end of your nose. What should you do? Well, you could stay at home and watch daytime TV, but seriously your best bet is to dab on a little medicated make-up and forget about it.
And remember, bad skin is not a losing battle. You will win in the end!

Sun protection

We all need to protect our skin from the sun's harmful rays. Not only does it age the skin, but it has played a role in the increased incidence of skin cancer.

But this doesn't mean you should hide indoors all the time. The sun's rays are not all bad. Sunlight helps create vitamin D. Just make sure you slap on a sunscreen that protects against both kinds of ultraviolet radiation from the sun—UVAs and UVBs—with a sun protection factor (SPF) of at least 15.

Keeping clean

Sweat is your body's way of cleansing and cooling itself naturally. You've always had sweat glands in your body, but thanks to puberty, these glands not only become super-active, they also begin to secrete different chemicals into the sweat, causing body odor. Androgens (those male hormones again) stimulate sweat and oil glands in the armpits, back, hands, feet, and vulva. And if that wasn't enough, you often find yourself even sweatier just before your period, due to your hormone levels being at their highest.

34

Keeping clean helps to keep bacteria and nasty odors at bay. So make sure you shower or bathe daily, using a mild soap. This will help wash away any bacteria.

Make sure you wear clean clothes every day. Try wearing clothes and underwear made of natural fibres like cotton, wool and silk which absorb and ventilate wetness much better than clothes made of other materials.

Deodorant or anti-perspirant. What's the difference?

Well, deodorants partially help cover the smell, but don't stop the sweating. Anti-perspirants actually stop perspiration before it starts.

As ever, which one you choose to use is completely down to personal choice. Both come in roll-ons, sticks, gels, sprays, and creams. Don't worry about which brand you buy, they're pretty much all the same. Be sure to read the instructions carefully. Some work better if you use them at night, while others should be put on in the morning.

Your hair

The hormones that create acne are the same ones that can make you feel like you're suddenly styling your hair with a brush that's been dipped in cooking oil. What's that about? Well, every single strand of hair on your head has its own sebaceous gland, which keeps your hair shiny and waterproof. But during puberty when these glands get super busy producing extra oil, it can make your hair feel greasier than ever.

Don't panic, there's plenty you can do! Washing your hair every day really helps. Use warm water and a small amount of shampoo. Don't scrub or rub too hard, as this can irritate your scalp and even damage your hair. After you've rinsed, use a conditioner specially formulated for greasy hair.

When styling your hair, be careful which products you use. Some styling gels or lotions can add extra grease, which defeats the whole purpose of washing it in the first place! Look for labels which say "oil free".

Everyone has body hair. We're born with a certain amount of it, but during puberty body hair grows in new (and sometimes embarrassing) places. In fact it might feel that nowhere on your body isn't growing hair. Coarser and usually darker hair starts to sprout in new places like your legs, and your underarms.

📖 Readers' stories

When I was twelve, I started growing hair on my legs. The boys in my class made fun of me constantly. But then my mom let me borrow some of her hair removal cream. I was so glad that I had spoken to her about it.
Emily, Atlanta

☑ Fact file

Hair grows in cycles. The average life span of a head hair is two to seven years. The average life span of an upper lip hair is four to five months.

Hair removal techniques

If you decide to get rid of this extra hair, there are a lot of choices out there. Here's the low-down on some of the techniques out there for you:

Tweezing/Plucking

What is it: Pulling hairs out one by one with a pair of tweezers.
Frequency: As needed. Once you tweeze a hair, it's gone for a month.
Cost: If you do it yourself, nothing. (Once you've bought the tweezers.)
Pain: Hurts for a second or two, especially in sensitive areas.
Pros: You do it yourself.
Cons: It can hurt at the time. But not for long.

Depilatory

What is it: A cream or gel that you put on the area where you want hair removed. It melts the hair roots, then you wash it off.
Frequency: Lasts a couple of weeks to a month.
Cost: Not expensive, from any good drugstore.
Pain: Can burn or irritate sensitive areas.
Pros: You do it yourself and the result is a very smooth area.
Cons: It can burn or leave the skin area red if the skin is sensitive.

Shaving

What is it: Using a razor to cut off hair right at the end.

Frequency: Daily to weekly depending how fast the hair grows.

Cost: Cost of razor and soap.

Pain: None (as long as you don't cut yourself!). Can cause some irritation.

Pros: You can do it yourself at any time.

Cons: Once you start shaving, hair grows back stubbly. Can cause ingrown hairs. Shaving rashes, shaving nicks, and other razor mishaps can cause discomfort.

Waxing

What is it: Spreading heated wax over the area where you want hair removed, letting it dry then pulling it off.

Frequency: Lasts four to six weeks.

Cost: If you do it at home not much more than depilatories. Having it done by a pro costs almost the amount of a hair cut.

Pain: Like ripping a bandage off a large area of skin. Some redness can follow.

Pros: Removes hair for up to a month or more.

Cons: Ripping hair out is very painful. Can be expensive.

Body image

Your body is where you live. And how you feel about it affects how you feel about yourself. Some of your attitude towards your body comes from what you put into it. But being healthy is only one part of the picture.

It's only natural to compare yourself to other girls, particularly your friends. But it's not always a good idea. After all, everyone develops differently at different times, and you might be ahead of or behind your friends. Puberty is usually toughest for those who develop first. And please, please don't compare yourself to celebrities and models. In reality, most people don't look like them. In fact most models don't look like they do in magazines either, those "perfect" bodies often owe more to retouching than nature!

Weight

Weight is probably the biggest obsession of our body-obsessed culture. Girls especially have a lot of anxiety about how much they weigh, how much they eat, and the general shape of their bodies. Eating well and exercising are the best ways to ensure your body weight is ideal for you.

Height

Height is another area that can make you feel self-conscious. Unfortunately, you can't control it, so you might as well learn to love it. Who says what's beautiful anyway? How you project your feelings about yourself is what really counts. As your body changes, work on having good posture and walk with a sense of confidence.

There's not much you can do about your height or development, but you can focus on the things that you really like about yourself. Maybe it's the color of your hair, or your smile, or the fact that you can always make people laugh. When you think about your friends, it's not the way they look that you care about, it's the people they are.

Body parts

And then there are specific body parts which us girls can't seem to stop obsessing about. You might think your stomach sticks out, but no one else even notices it.

Body parts come in all shapes and sizes, and with a little work and understanding it really is possible to love all of them. So give yourself a break and start rating, not hating yourself.

41

What boys think . . .

Most boys can't understand this constant drive girls have to obtain a perfect body shape. They think there are great looking petite skinny girls just as there are great-looking taller curvy girls. And you know what, they're absolutely right.

Believe it or not, boys don't just stare at one point of your anatomy. Yes, they may like looking at your breasts, but they honestly don't scrutinize girls the way we do. Boys look at the whole package —just as girls do with them. Come on, you don't just like someone solely because they've got a cute butt, do you! You like someone 'cause you find the whole package attractive—including their personality. Boys might love to tease girls about the way we look, but that's so they look cool in front of each other.

42

Your health

Food and exercise

One thing's for sure, you need to look after that precious body of yours. And you know what? Your body is very smart at letting you know how it feels. You just have to learn to listen to it.

The food groups

There's really no such thing as good food or bad food but the amount you eat of certain foods is important. Chocolate and cakes are fine if eaten occasionally and if you don't eat too much of them.

To make sure you're in tip-top shape, dig in to food from these five essential food groups every single day.

Carbohydrates

Examples: Bread, rice, pasta.
How much: six to eleven servings per day. (A serving is relatively small – one slice of bread and a half-cup of rice).

Fruit and vegetables

Examples: Green leafy vegetables like spinach and other greens. Root vegetables like carrots. Other vegetables like broccoli, cauliflower, the squash family, beans, aubergines, etc. Apples, pears, oranges, grapes, etc.
How much: At least three to five servings of vegetables and two to three servings of fruit a day.
        (A serving is about a half-cup.)

Dairy

Examples: Milk, yogurt, cheese.
How much: Two to three or more servings per day.
(A cup of milk is a serving.)

Protein

Examples: Meat, poultry, fish, dried beans, eggs, nuts.
How much: two to three servings per day. (A serving consists of one to three ounces of meat.)

✓ Fact file

Different vitamins do different things in your body. For example, vitamin C helps your body heal and fight infection. Vitamin A helps you see in the dark. Vitamin B helps give you more energy. There are tons of different vitamins – and you need to eat different fruits and vegetables to get them all.

More food!

Nutritionists recommend eating fats, oils, and sugar, in small amounts. This is because these foods are not only high in calories, they also have very little nutrition. So try to keep things like butter, cooking oil, candy, sugar and other sweeteners to a minimum. (Some fats, oils, and sugars are contained in other basic food categories. For example, both meat and dairy have fat, and fruit contains fructose, a kind of sugar.)

The more processed food is, the more likely it is to have a huge amount of sugar and fat. Processed foods include packaged cookies and snacks – basically, anything that's treated in an unnatural way to extend its shelf life.

Sugary foods are also very bad for your teeth, and finally – they can make you have energy rushes, then tired spells, rather than having lots of energy all day.

46

✅ Fact file

Fatty food increases your risk of having heart problems in later life. If you have lots of fat in your bloodstream from your diet, some of it can stick to the inside of your arteries (the pipes that carry your blood around your body). Less blood can flow through them, causing problems for your heart. If you eat less fatty food, you lower your risk of these problems happening to you when you're older.

The bottom line

Rather than dieting, focus on the type of food you're eating. Work on eating well and healthily. At the end of the day, you really are what you eat.

Whatever you do, don't be too strict with yourself. You'll take all the enjoyment out of eating. Which would be a real shame, food is awesome and one of the most pleasurable things there is. Learn to find a balance. Eat healthily, do some exercise, and eat chocolate!

Why is exercise important?

Exercise releases endorphins to your brain which make you feel good and happy. Not only that, but it's great for all your vital organs, keeping them strong and well. Plus, not only does your body become stronger and fitter, but exercise improves the quality of your skin, hair, and nails. With all that going on, what's not to love about exercise?

There are no set rules on how much exercise you need but 20 minutes of aerobic exercise at least three times a week is recommended.
Just remember to choose whatever type of exercise you find fun and enjoyable. Don't get hung up on calorie counting.

✓ Fact file

Aerobic exercise is any activity that raises your heart rate and speeds up your breathing.

What are the best types of exercise?

There are three main types of exercise and a mix of all three is most beneficial. These are the different types:

Stretching: This improves your body's flexibility and raises the heart rate slightly. Yoga and pilates are good stretching exercises.

Aerobic exercise: This is really good for your heart and lungs. Examples are: swimming, running, walking and dancing.

Strength and muscle building: This type of exercise builds muscle mass. The most efficient way to do this is through weight lifting. To see any results, you need to lift weights at least twice a week. If you're tempted to try this type of exercise, it's a good idea to get someone who knows what they're doing to give you some advice.

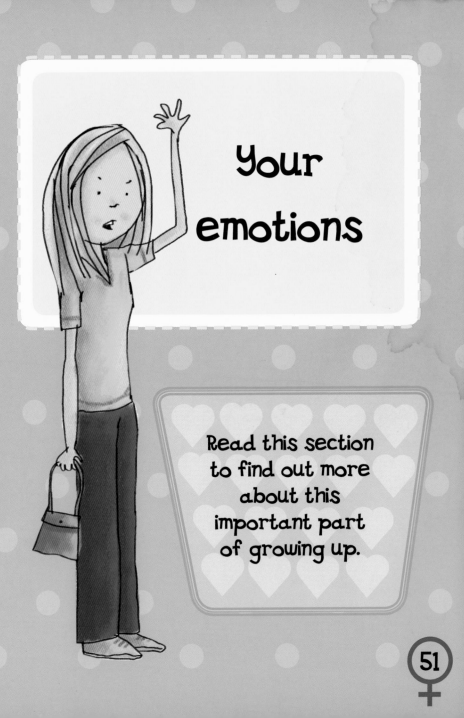

Your emotions

Read this section to find out more about this important part of growing up.

51

Your feelings

Your brain and the hormones it releases are responsible for all the changes happening in your body. As you grow into a more independent person, you and your brain must try to work out what's going on and the best way to respond. Every single person is different, which means you'll feel differently from other people too. Being aware of what you feel and trying to understand why, are ways of learning who you are.

✅ Fact file

People are moody. Teenagers are especially moody (just ask your parents!). Some of it has to do with hormones and some of it has to do with the life changes that go alongside, and some of it has to do with both! This means you are going to start experiencing feelings you've never felt before. And sometimes you're going to feel like you're on an emotional rollercoaster. Remember, you might not be able to control how you feel, but you can control what you do.

Here are just some of the emotions you might be experiencing right now:

⭐ Loneliness
Teenagers can often feel horribly lonely because your relationship to the world and the people around you is starting to change. Try and remember, everyone feels lonely from time to time. It's part of being human.

⭐ Anger
Anger is part of everyone's life and learning how to deal with it can be tough. But don't try to bury it. Working out safe, non-destructive ways to express your feelings is important to your health!

⭐ Jealousy
It's not nice, but everyone gets bitten by the green-eyed monster from time to time. But you can turn it on its head. Try to think about what you want in a positive way, e.g. if you're jealous of the way your best friend makes everyone laugh, don't feel bad about it. Instead, make a list of all the things you're good at. We all have special qualities. Learning to put a positive spin on things is so much better than wasting time on wanting what other people have.

★ Grief

When someone you know dies, it can have a huge impact on you. You're going to feel sadness, loss, anger, guilt, and sometimes anxiety about your own health.

Grieving takes time, energy, and patience. Everyone grieves in their own way and at their own pace. It's a good idea to talk to someone you trust about how you are feeling. Try to remember that eventually the intensity of the grief you are feeling will fade.

Grief isn't always linked to death either. The end of a friendship or relationship, or moving to a new home can spark feelings of grief.

★ Anxiety

This is a state of uneasiness about what the near or distant future might hold. Finding ways to relax can help. But if your anxiety is stopping you from being able to do everyday things, then talk to someone.

54

⭐ Mood swings
Moodiness goes hand in hand with being a teenager. Going from sadness to anger to joy in a matter of minutes can make you feel like you're seriously losing your grip. Sometimes it might be PMS or hormones causing it, other times it might just be life. If you feel like your feelings are totally out of control and you can't do anything to stop them, then please, talk to someone.

⭐ Self-esteem
You may suddenly find yourself becoming really down on yourself, believing you just don't measure up. Emotions like this can make us feel really bad about ourselves.

Try asking yourself why you're feeling like this. Try to understand what's stopping you from feeling good, and then focus on getting what you want. Don't let feelings of negativity stop you from enjoying your life. Recognize what you are good at and then find reasons to celebrate that.

⭐ Top tip

If any of your emotions get to the point where you feel you can't handle them, it's important to ask for help and try to figure out what's going on.

Who can I talk to?

If things seem too difficult, please ask for help. It doesn't matter who you ask—whether it's a friend, a sister or brother, a teacher or a parent. The most important thing is that it's someone you trust.

Right now, you are learning a lot about yourself, who you are and how you want to live your life. It's not just your body that changes during puberty, your mind is growing too. Some of your friendships are starting to deepen, some may well end, and the longstanding relationships you've had with people like your parents are going to change too. This is because you're starting to establish the unique identity and interests that will turn you into an independent, self-reliant adult.

At their best families are great, giving you unconditional love, comfort, and support. At their worst families can inflict huge amounts of pain, frustration, disappointment, and anger. For most of us, they're a little of both.

The best thing you can do is to keep talking to them. Try to talk about everyday stuff with your parents as a way of building a connection. This doesn't mean you have to tell them everything. The more you keep them informed about everyday things, even routine things like what you did in math today, the less they need to ask. Plus it shows your parents that you're mature and sensible enough to make good decisions.

★ Top tip

Writing your feelings down can really help you make sense of them. The simple act of putting it all down in words can help distance you from all the chaos and help you get some perspective and control. Keeping a diary can really help. Going back to read it later can help you figure out what makes you feel a certain way and why.

Expressing yourself

Talking about sensitive topics can be difficult. It's a good idea to plan what you want to say ahead of time. Write down the three most important things you want your parents to know. You may also want to think about how your parents might react and the best way to deal with it. It's important to get the person you want to speak with to give you their full attention. Try saying, "I want to talk to you about something important." This will prepare them for the conversation.

Also, try to approach them at a time when you know they'll be less busy. You might even ask them if they can put aside an hour at a particular time, so you know you've got their full attention.

Can I talk to you?

What's wrong?

⭐ Top tip

Some people find it easier to put their ideas down on paper. Give your note to your parents to read, then discuss it with them.

Sisters and brothers

Sisters and brothers can be frustrating, fun, annoying, and inspiring.

But think about it. Are you even half as nice to your siblings as you are to friends? If not, there's probably a reason why they aren't so nice back. It's hard to get along with someone who hogs the bathroom, the telephone, TV, computer, and parents' attention. Some fighting is inevitable. Obviously it's better to try and work things out by talking to each other. But if it becomes a pattern, let your parents' know.

My sister and I argue all the time. What can I do?

If you and your sister constantly bicker, try calling a truce. What's her favorite snack? Try making it for her, then sit down and have a friendly chat. Try spending time getting to know each other better.

It may be that you are jealous of her. If this is the case, talk to her about it. You'll probably find there are things about you she envies too.

Try not to let petty things get to you - life's too short!

59

Friends

As you grow up friends become more and more important. Girls know there's nothing better than hanging out with friends. Friends boost our self-esteem and teach us about ourselves. They help us get a grip on what's important in life – whether it's fun, loyalty, or honesty.

As you become more independent, your friends play a bigger part in your life. As school and other activities take you away from home, you may well spend more time with your friends than you do with your parents.

📖 Readers' stories

When I was thirteen, I remember my best friend got a new friend and I felt like the odd one out. I talked to them about it but they said I was being selfish so I decided to hang around with a different group. There were four of us so it made it easier to hang out as there was always someone around.

Anna, Chicago

Friendships can be made extra complicated by the fact that they're often part of a larger group. Sometimes it's hard to work out what you really want to do, and what you think your friends want you to think, do or be.

The pressure to do what everyone else is doing is huge. Giving in to dress a certain way is one thing, but going along with the crowd to drink or smoke is another.

 Top tip

Be kind first, instead of waiting to see if others will be nice to you.
If you don't know what to say, listen.
Remember, everyone likes to talk about themselves, so ask questions.

How to deal with it

No matter how wisely you pick your friends, sooner or later you're going to find yourself in a sticky peer pressure situation. If you feel uncomfortable with something it means it's wrong for you. Go with your gut feeling. It's all about becoming more self-reliant and learning more about who you are. And that's a good thing.

Good friends should never feel bad about saying no. But life isn't always that easy. Think of a few excuses you can use, so if you're in a sticky situation you're good to go.

If you're being bullied, don't suffer alone. Talk about it with an adult you trust. They might be able to help you decide what to do, or even find a way to stop the bullying. And remember, it's not your fault—no one deserves to be bullied.

How can I get her to change?

This is probably the hardest thing to do, but sometimes you realize that a friendship is not a good one, especially if it's causing you pain, worry, or upset. Be honest with yourself and your friend (that means talking to her, not complaining to everyone else about her). If it's really not in your best interests to hang on to a friend, then that's your cue to cut her loose. Take what you've learned from this friendship into your next one and make sure whoever you choose to give your friendship to, they return it one hundred percent.

⭐ **Top tip**

Make sure you speak up for a friend who's being pressured, and you can be sure they'll do the same for you. Just having one person stand with you against peer pressure makes it a lot easier to resist.

Romance

No one needs to have a boyfriend. There can be a lot of pressure from outside and even from yourself to be in a relationship. But it's just as cool to be on your own. You'll find a great sense of independence, freedom, and confidence.

Why certain people are attracted to each other is sometimes blindingly obvious and other times it's a complete mystery. But next time your friend falls for someone you wouldn't be seen dead with, don't fall on the floor laughing, instead remind yourself it's not all about looks. That's the amazing thing about love, there are no rules. Personality, common interests, humor, intelligence, all play a part. And all of us find different things attractive.

Crushes

Crushes can be amazing, but they can also be mind-numbingly, horrendously painful. They can range from mild to super-intense. Having a huge crush on someone (particularly if that person doesn't even know you exist) can sometimes feel like you've been squashed flat. Hey, it's not called a crush for no reason! You may want a crush to lead to something more, or you may not.

Is it love?

When you have a crush on someone, it can be hard to tell what that person is thinking. And the way you feel can seem to change from minute to minute. One moment you're on top of the world, the next you feel like sobbing into your pillow. It's all so intense, exciting and incredibly hard to sort out.

Trying to move from a crush or friendship phase into a romantic relationship can be tricky and confusing. It sure feels like love. But it's not love yet. It hasn't had time to grow into the closeness that's needed for love.

Embarrassment

One thing's for sure, you won't get through puberty without a few blushes.

Why do we blush?

It's all about biology. When your body is faced with something that might be cringe-worthy, it doesn't know whether to tough it out or leg it. Your mind wants to up and leave really quick, but your legs have other ideas. So to try and get you moving, the mind rushes blood to your muscles to make them faster and stronger. Some of this blood goes to your face and that explains the redness.

 ## Top tip

Laugh at yourself.
Just shrug your shoulders and laugh as if you love nothing better than making an idiot of yourself.

 66

Banishing your blushes

Sadly, there's no magic cure
for blushing, but there are
a few things you can
do to try and lessen the
embarrassment . . .

✪ Don't think about it.
Next time you feel
your cheeks getting
hot and red, start
to think about
something else. Try to
remember a date from your history lessons, or work out a
math problem. Before you know it, your blushes will have
totally faded.

✪ Create a distraction.
Talk about something else. If everyone else sees you acting
like you're not bothered, they won't care either.

✪ It happens to everybody.
Remember, cringe-making stuff happens to everyone,
including celebrities. So hold your head up high, you're in a
cool club.

✪ Stay calm.
Breathe properly and don't stress about the situation.
It's really not as bad as you think.

How would you deal with it?

Take this quiz to find out:

1. Your mom puts up a banner outside the house, saying "Congratulations! You're a woman now!" to celebrate your first period. What do you say?

a. "Mom! How could you?" Then plonk yourself down on the sofa with your arms crossed and a face like thunder.

b. "Oh, Mom. Periods are so last year."

c. "Just wait till your 40th, Mom. I'll get you back!"

2. You've started at a new school and some girls come over to talk to you. How do you react?

a. You can't speak. You gaze at them open-mouthed.

B. You exclaim: "Wow! Do you like me? Shall we hang out at lunch, then you could come to my house later and we could all walk to school together tomorrow!"

C. You say "Hi!" and are friendly.

3. Your friends are at the door. Your mom comments on how nice your bra looks under your sweater. What do you do?

a. Throw a fit and shout at your mom, "You're so embarrassing. I hate you!" before stomping off.

b. You make a great show of hoisting up the straps and parade around, striking poses.

c. You say, "Thanks, Mom. I quite like it too."

4. You're at school when you drop your bag and a tampon rolls out across the floor in front of everyone. How do you react?

a. You run out of the school, all the way back home.

b. One by one everyone starts laughing. You join in.

c. You say calmly, "Oops! Thank goodness it wasn't a used one!" You then pick it up and act like nothing happened.

5. Your dad insists on singing a song in front of your friends. Do you...

a. Stand still in the doorway, cringing with embarrassment, unable to move or to speak.

b. You shriek, "Isn't my dad great!"

c. Say, "Don't worry Dad, practice makes perfect."

Do you deal or squeal? Turn the page to find out . . .

Answers

Mostly a

Try to relax more. Remember that running away from a problem might be effective, but it's not cool and it certainly doesn't solve anything. And just maybe things aren't quite as cringeworthy or dreadful as you think they are.

Mostly b

You usually bluff your way out of potentially embarrassing situations by acting like a fool. You like to do things for a laugh. Humor is a great way out of any situation, but just make sure you don't use it to embarrass others.

Mostly c

Wow! You really know how to deal with the most awful situations that life has to throw at you. You may not need this chapter, but why not read it anyway. You might even pick up some tips to add to your repertoire.

How can I feel less embarrassed?

Everyone has doubts and insecurities. Even if they don't show them.

As you get more used to the embarrassing situations life is determined to throw at you, you will become more successful in keeping your cool. No matter how embarrassing a situation, no doubt someone, somewhere shares your shame.

The first rule of cool: It's not what you do it's the way that you do it.
The second rule of cool: Regain your composure, quickly and calmly.
The third rule of cool: Don't try too hard to impress. You could end up being more fool than cool!

☆ Top tip

Wrong way of thinking about an embarrassing incident. "I feel so stupid. I hate myself. Everyone must think I'm so dumb etc."

Right way of thinking about an embarrassing incident. "Oh well, I don't suppose it was such a big deal. Everyone's probably forgotten about it already." Armed with this attitude, you'll get through anything.

Here are some more tips to help you feel less embarrassed:

⭐ Be a trendsetter: You've dashed over to your friend's house. She answers the door and says "Nice outfit!" That's when you realize your shirt's undone and you're flashing your bra. Simply smile back and say, "Yeah, cool isn't it!" Act confident, even when you mess up, and you can get away with anything.

⭐ Act silly: Popular people are never scared to do silly things. So next time you walk into a classroom to find everyone giggling because you've got toilet paper stuck to your shoe, just wink and give them a smile. It shows you don't take yourself too seriously.

⭐ Love yourself: Sometimes it's hard to shrug off those feelings of shame. But next time you have to go to a party with a huge zit on your nose, don't spend the whole evening hiding in the corner, cringing. Keep a happiness diary instead. Every time you get a compliment or do something well, jot it down and you can flick back any time to remind yourself how utterly great you are.

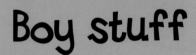

Boy stuff

They look different.
They talk different.
They think different!

One of the effects of puberty is that you'll start noticing the opposite sex a little more. So read on for the inside scoop on boys . . .

73

It's different for boys

Boys worry about the changes they are going through as much as you do and they share many of the same issues.

They usually start puberty somewhere between the ages of 11 and 14. This is often a little later than girls, but they will soon catch up!

All the changes for boys happen on the inside to begin with, when their testicles start producing male sex hormones. Here is a list of the main changes for boys:

- ✪ Facial hair grows
- ✪ Penis grows larger and longer
- ✪ Height and weight increase
- ✪ Voice 'cracks' as it becomes deeper
- ✪ They grow body hair including pubic and underarm hair
- ✪ Body sweats more
- ✪ Shoulders and chest get bigger
- ✪ Hair and skin become oily
- ✪ Hands and feet get larger

Boys have issues with body hair too. Although generally they don't tend to remove theirs. They grow hair on their arms and legs and sometimes on their chest and stomach.

Pubic hair grows around their penis and testicles and grows in their armpits.

Facial hair grows and at some point they might want to start shaving, which they do with electric razors or by wet shaving with soap and water.

☑ Fact file

When a boy's voice cracks it means it sounds deeper than it did before. When boys go through puberty, their larynx gets much larger, and becomes visible as a lump in their throat. This lump is called an Adam's apple, and their bigger larynx gives them a deeper voice.

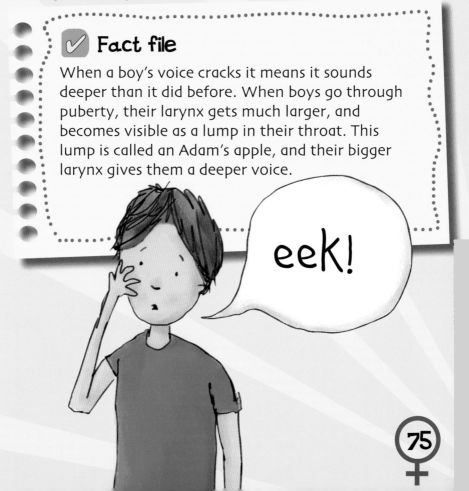

eek!

75

On the inside

One place where boys notice changes happening is between their legs.

Behind the scenes there are lots of changes at work. Boys' testicles will start to produce sperm. And their penis will start to get hard and point upwards from time to time – this is called an erection. Below is a diagram of a penis, with all the behind-the-scenes stuff marked on it.

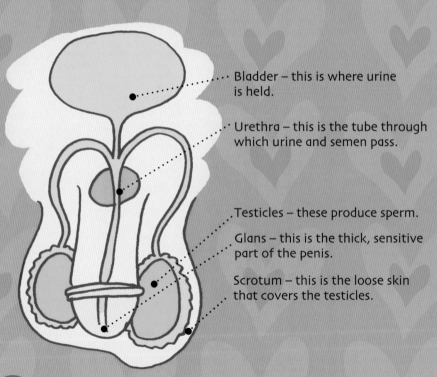

Bladder – this is where urine is held.

Urethra – this is the tube through which urine and semen pass.

Testicles – these produce sperm.

Glans – this is the thick, sensitive part of the penis.

Scrotum – this is the loose skin that covers the testicles.

Boy get erections when blood rushes into their penis and fills up all the spaces in it. Muscles around the penis tighten to hold in all this extra blood.

Boys find themselves having erections at the weirdest times and in the oddest places and it can be really embarrassing for them. However, it's all perfectly normal and it's just one of the new sensations of puberty.

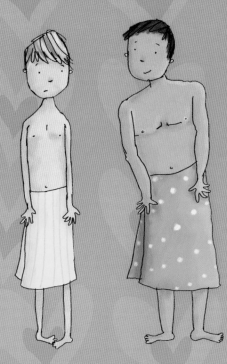

Most boys worry about the size of their penis, particularly during puberty, but in fact, most adult erect penises are about the same size. The process can be very slow and it can take a year or so to notice any change after the testicles have grown.

Lots of boys boast about the size of their penises and much of that is wishful thinking!

One of the effects of puberty is that you begin to like boys more. Of course, this doesn't mean you'll wake up one morning desperate to find yourself a boyfriend. But it does mean that you'll stop finding them so annoying, and you will probably start enjoying hanging out with them and making friends with them.

Readers' stories

I had been friends with the boy next door for years – since we were about four years old. But when I started going through puberty, I began to think I really liked him. I became totally awkward around him whenever he came over—we used to talk for hours. It's only when I overheard him telling a friend that I was being really strange that I snapped out of it and started treating him normally again. He must still wonder why I was behaving so oddly, though!

Megan, Cleveland

Help!
Got a
problem?

Whatever your problem, the answers are in this section . . .

Q. All my friends tease me and say I have a crush on my math teacher. He is my favorite teacher and I do like him a lot but how can I stop these rumors from spreading? I'd die if he heard them!

A. Try not to worry about this too much. All girls have crushes on teachers – male and female. It's just a stage you go through, when you have a need for someone or something to be the object of your affections. It's perfectly normal. When your friends tease you, either ignore them or laugh about it with them. You can joke that yes, you did have a crush on him, but now you're far too mature for that kind of thing and besides, what about the age difference?

As you get older, you'll learn that nobody's perfect, even the people you idolize. And you may even begin to like people the same age as you.

Q. My best friend and I were friends for the whole time we were at elementary school. But now we're at junior high, she has started being nasty to me, and tells me what to do all the time. She's started hanging out with different girls and they all seem to laugh at me. She whispers things to her new friends and I'm sure they're talking about me. What shall I do?

A. Unfortunately, when you start a new school, it often happens that old friends may change for no real reason. Maybe your friend just wants to make new friends and keep you at a distance for a while. Rather than worrying about this, you can make new friends too.
Put all your energy into meeting new girls who you have something in common with. Try not to worry about your old best friend. You can keep her at a distance too for a while. When she sees how popular you are with your new friends, she may come around in the end. And even if she doesn't, your other friends will be there instead.

Q. My family has just moved to a new house, and I've started a new school. I'm really shy and finding it hard to make new friends.

A. This is a difficult situation for anyone finding herself in a new setting. It can be really difficult to make the first approach to a group of strangers. You need a lot of courage. Take a deep breath, and just go up to a group of girls, introduce yourself and see what happens. One good way of making friends is to join an after-school club such as drama. Acting is a good way of overcoming your shyness and you're bound to make new friends in the process.

Q. I'm worried about my friend. Everything she eats, she makes herself throw up. I've tried to tell her to stop doing it but she won't. She says she is worried that she is fat. What can I do?

A. You are right to be worried about your friend and it's good that you are caring about her. She may be suffering from bulimia, which is a serious eating disorder. You must tell a trusted adult immediately. Talk to your parents, a school teacher or another adult you trust. Your friend needs love and support. She may feel that you have betrayed her trust but be patient and stand by her. Eventually she'll see that you helped her and that you really care about her.

Q. It's really easy for me to walk home from school as I only live less than a mile away. Tons of my friends walk home. But my mom always insists on picking me up in the car. How can I persuade her to let me walk home from school?

A. Maybe the first step would be for you to ask your mom to walk to the school to pick you up. You could then both walk home which would give you both some exercise and save on adding to the traffic at the same time! Only when your mom is convinced that you are safe will she let you walk home on your own. If you have a school friend who lives nearby, you could both walk to and from school together. That would probably put your mom's mind at rest. Talk to your mom and see what she thinks of these ideas. I'm sure you'll find a compromise, but don't push too hard. Sometimes being patient is the best way.

Q. I'm really tall for my age and I'm much taller than my boyfriend is. We're both 13 and sometimes I can hear people at school laughing behind our backs and calling us "Little and Large".

A. Please don't worry about this. Your boyfriend obviously doesn't mind. All boys and girls grow at different rates. Some people stop growing at 12, some don't stop growing till they are 20 or more. Some of your friends and even your boyfriend might catch you up one day. But does it really matter? You should be pleased you're so tall.

85

Q. I have a problem with pimples. I've tried every face cream and lotion possible and I can't get rid of them. I eat a healthy diet and drink lots of water but nothing seems to help. They are really bad. What can I do?

A. The truth is you may not be able to get rid of them completely. If your pimples are really bad then talk to your doctor to see what he or she recommends. It may be that you need some special medication to help cure your pimples.

Most of your friends will be getting pimples too and the good thing is that most acne clears up in the late teen years.

Q. What if my period starts when I'm out and about and I don't have a pad or tampon. Will it show on my clothes?

A. If you get caught out then don't worry. Try to make a temporary pad out of folded toilet tissue. If you can, then ask a teacher or the school nurse or a friend if they have a spare one.

So that you feel more comfortable, tie a sweater around your waist to make a cover up but the chances are nobody will notice anything!

Q. My parents are divorced. Every weekend I go and stay with my dad but I hate my stepmom. I can't bear her. She's always sucking up to my dad, but she's pretending. Underneath it all she makes him do exactly what she wants. And he's always buying her presents. I hate her so much.

A. It's very difficult to form a good relationship with your step-parents. But you are going to have to take a deep breath and try to get along with her. Your feelings of jealously towards her are totally understandable but try and get along with her for your dad's sake. She must have some good qualities, or your dad wouldn't have married her.

If you really find things don't improve, try having a quiet word with your dad and see if you can come up with other solutions.

Q. I'm always eating junk food. I'm thin now but I'm worried I might get fat. How can I stop eating food which is bad for me.

A. Eating junk food every now and then isn't a disaster, you need to make sure that you balance it out with food which is good for you.

Try cutting down the junk food gradually. It'll be easier than trying to give up altogether. Find some healthy snack foods that you enjoy eating but remember it's easier to allow yourself a treat every now and then than to stick to a junk-food-free diet

Q. I'm really flat chested. All my friends have big breasts but mine are really small. They are always talking about bras and I feel left out as I don't have one.

A. It's hard not to compare yourself to your friends but remember for every girl who is worried that hers are too small, there is another girl who is upset because hers have grown quickly and are too big.

Your body has a schedule of its own and your breasts may increase in size in the near future.

Choose outfits which make you feel comfortable and confident. You are lucky to be able to go bra-less and clothes often fit better on smaller chests.

Q. There's a boy in the year ahead of me who I really like and I think he likes me. But I'm too scared to make the first move and I don't understand why he doesn't say anything to me about it. Help!

A. Boys find approaching girls really hard. He's probably just as shy as you are. A lot of people hide their feelings because they're scared of rejection. There's no reason why a girl shouldn't approach a boy first. There's no rule that says it has to be the boy who makes the first move. Most boys really like it when a girl does. It means the girl must really like them. The first thing to do is to make friends with this boy. So try to summon up the courage to speak to him. Once you've made the first move, it won't be so difficult. Perhaps suggest that a few of you go to the movies. Once you feel relaxed with each other, there may even be romance in the air!

Glossary

Stuff you might hear, see, or read – and what it means!

acne
Acne is a condition that affects your skin, making it very pimply and red. It is treatable, though, so if you think you might have it, go and see your doctor.

bacteria
Microscopic life forms. Some are harmful to us and some are healthy.

blackhead
A type of pimple, where a black dot is visible on the tip of the pimple. Caused by some dirt blocking one of the pores on your skin.

cells
The smallest units of life. All living things are made of cells. Some such as BACTERIA may have just one cell.

deodorant
Nice-smelling stuff that you can spray yourself with after you shower, to stop you smelling .You can also get deodorant you roll on to your skin.

estrogen
A female sex hormone.

gender
Your sex - whether you are male or female.

genitals
Genitals is a term that is used for the "sex organs'" of both men and women. So, a man's penis and testicles, or a woman's vagina.

hormones
The chemicals in your body that cause you to grow and change shape during puberty.

mood swing
When you find you are alternately very energetic and happy, then rather down and moody. Mood swings are a side-effect of the hormones in your body, and are perfectly normal.

monthly cycle
The number of days from one period to the next.

ovaries
These are the organs in a woman that produce an egg every month.

pad
An absorbent paper towel that women place in their underwear during their period. It soaks up the blood, allowing them to get on with their normal activities.

peer pressure
This is a term that describes the pressure that your friends or classmates might put on you to do something you aren't comfortable with.

period
If a woman's egg isn't fertilized, it is flushed out of her body. The soft layer that lines her womb is flushed out at the same time, leading to a discharge from her vagina. This is her period, and lasts for a few days every month.

pimples
Pimples on your skin are caused by dirt and grease blocking your pores.
They are most common on the face and neck, but can appear elsewhere too, like your arms and back.

pore
The tiny holes in your skin. They can get blocked up with dirt and grease to cause pimples.

premenstrual syndrome (PMS)
This is the term that describes the emotional time many women go through just before or during the start of their period.

puberty
This is the term that describes all of the physical changes a boy goes through to become a man – and the changes a girl goes through to become a woman.

pubic hair
Hair that grows around the external sex organs.

sperm
The male sex cell produced in the testicles.

tampon

A small tube of absorbent material that women can use instead of pads to soak up the blood during their periods.

testosterone

A male sex hormone.

toxic shock syndrome

A bacterial infection that can be caused by wearing a tampon for too long without changing it.

95

Index